Maxie
and the
Axolotl

Heather Hughes

Illustrated by Brian Rivera

To order additional copies of this book, contact:
Xlibris
0800-056-3182
www.xlibrispublishing.co.uk
Orders@ Xlibrispublishing.co.uk

ISBN: Softcover   978-1-9845-9362-7
        EBook   978-1-9845-9361-0

Print information available on the last page

Rev. date: 02/29/2020

Maxie and the Axolotl

DEDICATION

For Kevin, Lindsay, David and their children.

Maxie lived near an enormous lake
She would often visit during her break

Put on her hat to protect from the sun
She felt in her bones today would bring fun

Maxie walked to the lake and sat on a ledge
She opened her lunch bag to reveal lovely veg

There was chicken and nachos and water to drink
About to tuck in, well as you would think…

At the water's edge, something disturbed
She went to look, though not perturbed

As she peered in the water, she didn't believe
Exactly what it was that her eyes perceived.

There in the water, what could it be?
Her own image that she could see?

When she moved to the left, it moved to the right
Was the flickering shadows playing tricks with her sight?

She immediately jumped back in curious surprise
What was it she saw before her very eyes?

It's face was like hers with bunches and a wide smile
Although with four legs and a tale all the while

An amphibian, of course, as it crawled to the ledge
Though eyesight was poor, he could smell the veg

It wasn't the veg he wanted to eat
But her chicken would make a tasty treat

What could she do to befriend the creature?
Who seemed quite at home and pleased to meet her

This new found friend was an Axolotl
who was sucking the chicken and water from the bottle

His body was soft with feathery gills
Living mainly in water eating fish for his meals

So they sat in the shade as he liked dim lights
Filling their faces with all the delights

When they were done, he crawled on her lap
Looked up to her face and gave it a tap

"Thank you" he said, "now fetch a large vessel"
"fill it with water if that is no hassle"

"I'd like to come with you and see where you play"
"and if it is possible, stay for the day"

She took off her hat and put 'Axo' within
To fetch a container to put the carnivore in

When it was full, he swam round and round
Pleased to be back on familiar ground

By now it was time to return to the lake
Best to get back for both of their sake

An extraordinary adventure, they both agreed
They would do it again…oh yes, guaranteed!

Printed in the United States
By Bookmasters

"Where will you take me in this fine abode?"
So off to the park, Maxie merrily strode

They slid down the slide and swung on the swing
Whizzed on the round-about, did everything